Exeter's West Quarter

&

Adjacent Areas

PETER THOMAS

From the Archives of
The Isca Historical Photographic Collection
(Established 1974)

Printed and bound in Great Britain

Copyright © Peter David Thomas 2008

ISBN 0-9516820-4-0
EAN 9780951682043

British Library Cataloguing in Publication Data
A catalogue record for this book is available from The British Library

Concept, design and production
Peter Thomas

Published by
THOMAS CASTLE
5 Abbey Road, Exeter, Devon EX4 7BG

The Isca Historical Photographic Collection
(Established 1974)
www.iscacollection.co.uk

The Isca Collection, established in 1974 to preserve the studio negative stock of The Henry Wykes Studio of Northernhay Place, Exeter is the largest private historical photo archive relating to the City of Exeter. The original work of the Wykes Studio covers many aspects of life in the city, street scenes, industry, shop fronts, aerial views, dignitaries, events, private houses, royalty, weddings and hundreds of portraits of local people and families.

The Collection has been greatly expanded over a period of 30 years and contains some of the rarest and early Exeter photographs. Privately owned by photographer and local historian Peter Thomas it is suggested that the Isca Collection now contains over 60,000 images. It also includes an extensive collection of modern material on Exeter, Devon and Dorset.

The Isca collection has formed the basis for many of Exeter's local history books, videos, dvd's and major exhibitions. Assistance has been given to the media on numerous occasions for documentaries, radio broadcasts, theatrical productions, articles and other activities.

Acknowledgements
Sincere thanks is given to the following people for their help with this book

The late Mr F Collins, Mrs S Cox, Mr B Gowlett, Mr & Mrs Pearce, Mr J Parkin, The late Mr W Brewer,
The late Arthur Everett, Mrs Hill, The Phillips family, Mr K White, Mrs L Till,
The Westcountry Studies Library

The Isca Collection would like to thank all those who have supported its work over the last 34 years

EXETER'S WEST QUARTER
&
ADJACENT AREAS

The West Quarter is for many Exonians, the essence of old Exeter and still retains some aspects of old-world charm but is now greatly diminished and changed. The purpose of this book is to bring together for the first time a series of fascinating and rare photos that will help to capture the atmosphere and historical nature of the west side of the city that is now almost forgotten. This area of Exeter is one of the most historically interesting and reflects on the early origins of the city.

The walled city as we know it today, of which approximately 75% still stands, was built by the Romans after their invasion around 50 AD. They were to construct a stone town wall 150 years later incorporating gateways on the East, North, West and South sides. The geology of the city's west side consisted of natural coombes and red sandstone cliffs offering good protection. It was on the west side that a simple entry was made – The West Gate. Early references describe it as "a mean structure" as it did not have the grandeur or significance of the other city gates. A further gate was also to be built that led down to the Quay known as the Water Gate. Its purpose was to control access to the Quay in order to protect the area and the valuable merchandise stored there. Extensive marshland extended across the flood plain westward, with a wide tidal river system leading directly to the sea. The marshlands on the west side were drained and in the 12th century leats constructed off the river to power mills used for grinding corn, tanning and for fulling or tucking part of the production process for woollen cloth. This latter trade was mostly situated around the immediate vicinity of West Gate. The land known as Shilhay may have formed over the centuries as a natural feature created by the river system. The name Shilhay could originate from the word "shillet" being decomposed rock from a cliff of which there are extensive cliffs at Mount Dinham a short distance up river. Early maps show Shilhay as an area used in the 17th and 18th centuries for the drying of woollen cloth which was attached to wooden racks by tenter hooks. The cloth trade brought great wealth to Exeter. Further uses for the Shilhay were for depositing coal and timber drying. It was to become an extensive industrial area in the 19th and 20 the centuries.

Exeter Quay was to evolve as a natural progression over the centuries but greatly expanded in Elizabethan times with the building of a remodelled and extended Quay and grand Custom House. Further expansion took place in the 19th century with the construction of fine warehouses. Passage across the river has traditionally been carried out by hand pulled ferry, known as a floating bridge, since the early 17th century and the service continues today. The Exeter Ship Canal built in 1564 by-passed the river and was responsible for bringing further wealth to the city with the importing and exporting of goods. In 1830 a Basin was constructed at the head of the canal to accommodate a larger number of commercial vessels. At the turn of the twentieth century Exeter's Electricity Generating Station was built at the Basin to power the new Electric Trams that operated in the city from 1905 until 1931.

Exe Island, also evolved from drained land, became a site for a number of businesses in the 19th and twentieth centuries including a foundry, gas works, smithy, council yard, timber storage and a slaughter house. The area also included a number of small cottages, pubs and a school for local children. The only known photo of Exe Island School is shown, together with Paradise School off Bartholomew Terrace and Central School with scenes from the playground. An imposing Mission building and chapel together with a Lodging House dominated the central area. An unusual entry to Exe Island was from Frog Street under a stone arch in the New Bridge Street viaduct.

In Bonhay Road farmers, drovers and shepherds would congregate whilst visiting the Cattle Market taking time to visit the local pub. It was here, at Bonhay, that the city's last working horses were sold.

Throughout the centuries merchants and businessmen have owned properties on the west side of the city. This is borne out by some fine timber framed properties that are still to be seen. Local workers lived close to their place of work but their living conditions were often that of the impoverished. This is particularly relevant to the out break of Cholera in 1832 when squalid conditions caused the death of many people in the area. In the late 1920s properties around the West Gate and Stepcote Hill could be seen in semi-derelict state. The conditions instigated a major slum clearance scheme in 1930. A remarkable series of photos, taken in 1928, shows the Stepcote Hill area before any changes occurred. The West Quarter and adjacent areas was a strong hold for local families particularly around the area of Stepcote Hill and its adjacent streets. Children often played on the steps of Stepcote Hill and people would gather under the gas lamp installed at the junction beside St Mary steps Church. Here you will see children, horse drawn dust carts, donkey and carts and street sellers. The area contained ancient buildings and narrow lanes and alleys where traditional trades took place. Off Coombe Street were the Public Baths and Wash House. A unique painting by the Exeter artist John Shapland shows two local ladies undertaking their washing whilst having a good gossip.

A significant event took place in 1961 when an early 15th century building was lifted up and moved adjacent to the West Gate site. It had stood in the way of the construction of Western Way inner by pass but was saved by a preservation order. Today it is known as The House that moved.

This book will give for the first time an overall view of this most historic and evocative side of the City of Exeter. The West Quarter and adjacent areas have been a fundamental aspect of Exeter's industrial and historical development being integrated into the very essence of Exeter's local communities. For many of us who have been familiar with these areas it has a special place in our affections and regret that some of Exeter's most interesting and historical aspects have been swept away. The photographs will however record EXETER'S WEST QUARTER & ADJACENT AREAS for future generations.

Peter Thomas
Exeter
2008

CHAPTERS

Front cover   West Street *c* 1900
Back cover   John Rocque map 1744

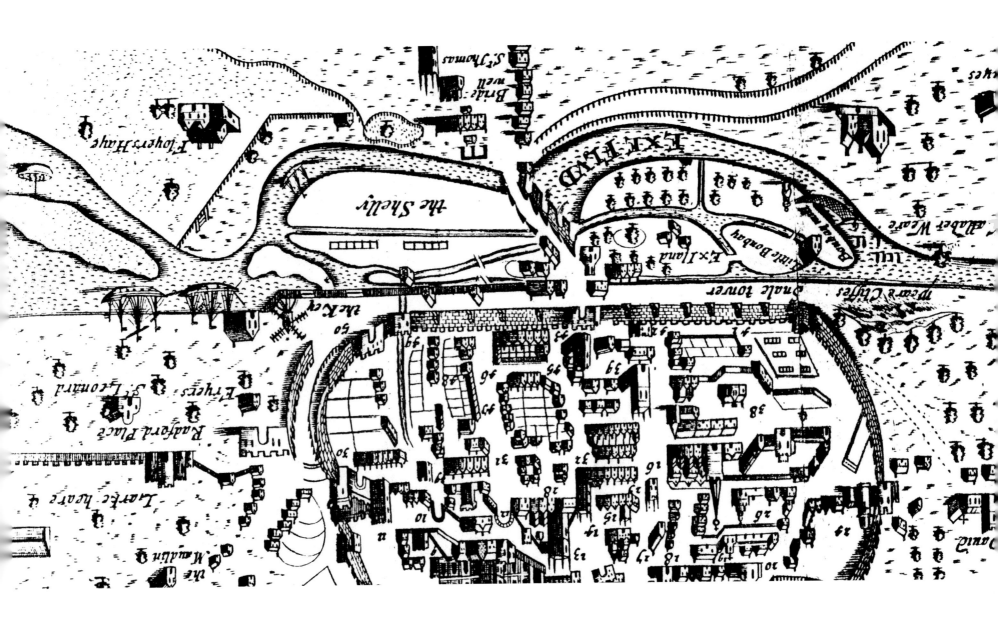